THE AQUA
PERSONALITY

January 21 to February 19

A Portrait by Roy McKie

Collins: London and Glasgow

Aquarians are keenly interested in world affairs,

are not impressed by grandeur

and learn well from others.

They are more loving to people in general

than to individuals.

They tend to be impractical,

are dreamers

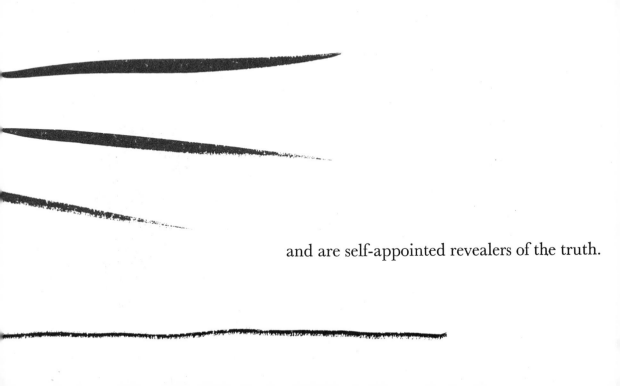

and are self-appointed revealers of the truth.

They delight in shocking,

treat children as equals,

are cool and detached

but resent criticism.

They make great plans,

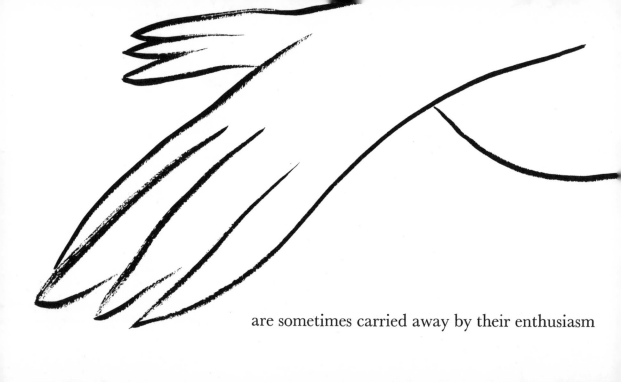

are sometimes carried away by their enthusiasm

and often have cold hands and feet.

They have an inventive genius,

are extremely independent

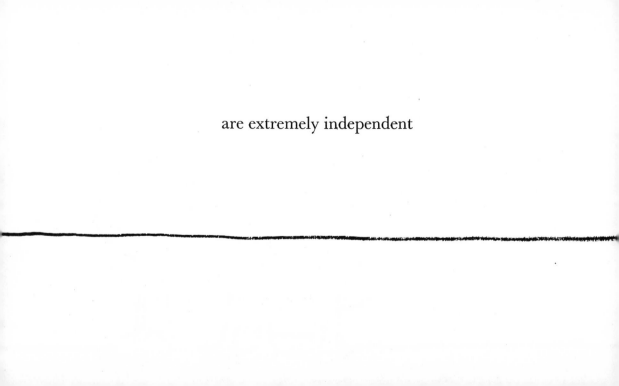

and are always eager to try something new.

They get along well with people both at work

and at play,

are loyal